"*One Like Silence* is a song of wisdom sung by a mature singer reflecting various sources of inspiration: experience, myth, sacred texts, and so many other living details that distinguish and distract us on our journeys. These poems satisfy the poet's quest for wholeness; moreover, they are a gift to any seeker who, like Chris Ellery, finds deep purpose sung with lyrical beauty."

—KEN HADA,
author of *Come before Winter*

"The reading of this book leaves me stunned and falling in love all over again with the power of words. Chris Ellery's poetry is nothing less than divine, with a wisdom Seamus Heaney himself would have wished he had written. It leaves us breathless, wanting to split ourselves open to become one with this beautiful earth."

—KARLA K. MORTON,
2010 Texas State poet laureate

"In the poem 'Provision': 'Consider the bowl of the body.' This poem attempts to define ownership using objects from the mundane to the holy. The questions in this poem—'the bounteous marrow of this poverty'—are answered by the rest of the book. There is, ultimately, much to be thankful for, after much 'dangerous and determined love,' (something incredibly human and exquisitely put), that yes, we need to consider, and own, the bowl of our temporal and spiritual body. Few books have this much wisdom."

—ALAN BIRKELBACH,
2005 Texas State poet laureate

ONE LIKE SILENCE

ONE LIKE SILENCE

CHRIS ELLERY

RESOURCE *Publications* • Eugene, Oregon

ONE LIKE SILENCE

Resource Publications
An Imprint of Wipf and Stock Publishers
199 W. 8th Ave., Suite 3
Eugene, OR 97401

www.wipfandstock.com

PAPERBACK ISBN: 979-8-3852-2247-6
HARDCOVER ISBN: 979-8-3852-2248-3
EBOOK ISBN: 979-8-3852-2249-0

06/25/24

for all the children
every avatar triumphant

with love
gratitude
and joy

One Nature, perfect and pervading, circulates in all natures,

One Reality, all-comprehensive, contains within itself all realities.

The one Moon reflects itself wherever there is a sheet of water,

And all the moons in all the waters are embraced within the one Moon.

Yongjia Xuanjue, *Song of Enlightenment*

We must find out how to get everything back into connection with everything else.

Carl Jung, BBC Interview

CONTENTS

Acknowledgements | xi

Prologue: Unifying Theory | 1

OUT OF THE BLACKNESS ECSTATIC

Rain | 5

A Recollection of Evolution in Scuba Diving Class | 6

Kali | 8

Secret Place | 9

Wheels | 10

Calf | 11

Lightning | 12

Live Alive Life Lived Lives Living | 13

One-Handed Tree | 14

Double Feature | 15

THE RIVER OF AFFIRMATION AND JOY

Bodhi | 19

Ashes | 20

Cradleboard | 21

Escaping Childhood Trauma | 23

Happily Ever After | 25

Flames | 26

Charity | 27

Making Bread on the Fourth of July | 29

Silent | 31

The River of Affirmation and Joy | 32

MOON IN A MUDDY ARROYO

Eris, Mother of Manslaughter | 37

North and South | 38

Spit | 41

Samaritan | 43

A Fence Got Tired of Being a Fence | 45

Hillel | 46

Every Beautiful Name | 47

Bread | 52

Crossroads | 53

WASP Man, OR Bodies of Protest and Justice | 54

ENCHANTED ROCK

Canyon's Counsel | 65

Mandala | 66

Headwaters | 68

Ecologue | 70

Horse Horses Horseman | 72

Nomad | 74

Aaron | 76

Juvenile | 78

Isle | 79

Shamanic | 80

THE ORDEAL OF MARRIAGE

Star and Ditch | 85

Play Mates | 86

The Wheel of Maya | 88

Harrison, Arkansas | 89

Arachnid | 91

A Small Blue Flame | 92

Ruth | 94

Provision | 95

We Went for a Drive | 96

Phone | 98

HARMONY OF STAR AND DITCH

Aquifer | 101

Now Is Always | 102

After Reading Some Late Poems of Pablo Neruda | 103

Zophar | 105

Present | 107

Weightless | 108

Of Form and the Formless | 109

Daughter Heaven Mountain | 110

The Lake of Serenity | 113

The Path of Love beyond Love | 114

ACKNOWLEDGEMENTS

The author is grateful to the editors and publishers of the following journals and anthologies in which some of these poems originally appeared:

A Fire to Light Our Tongues: "Calf"

Blue Hole: "Juvenile"

Book of Matches: "Charity" and "Samaritan"

Christian Century: "Of Form and the Formless"

Crosswinds Poetry Journal: "Rain" and "Star and Ditch"

divot: "Now Is Always"

Phi Kappa Phi Forum: "Bread"

Speckled Trout: "Harrison, Arkansas"

The Chest: Journal of the American College of Chest Physicians: "A Recollection of Evolution in Scuba Diving Class" and "Flames"

The Power of the Pause (A Wising Up Anthology): "Silent" and "A Small Blue Flame"

The Windhover: "Hillel" and "Lightning"

Voices of Resilience: "Crossroads"

West Texas Literary Review: "Aaron" and "Live Alive Life Lived Lives Living"

Wholeness (A Wising Up Anthology): "Every Beautiful Name"

Windward Review: "A Fence Got Tired of Being a Fence" and "Spit"

Writing Texas: "The Wheel of Maya," "Aquifer," and "Unifying Theory"

"After Reading Some Late Poems by Pablo Neruda" appeared in the National Poetry Month issue of *Poets for Human Rights* and was reprinted in *The Sailors Review*.

"Rain" was a finalist for the Crosswinds Poetry Award.

"The Wheel of Maya" received the Texas Poetry Award from the Texas Association of Creative Writing Teachers.

"Secret Place," Double Feature," "Cradleboard," "Making Bread on the Fourth of July" (as "Baking in Quarantine"), "Mandala" (as "Geometric"), "Headwaters," "Provision," "Zophar," and "Daughter Heaven Mountain" were written in response to prompts posted at Texas Poetry Assignment and appear on the TPA website (texaspoetryassignment.org). "Zophar" was published in *Lone Star Poetry*, an anthology of poems from the first year of TPA. Many thanks to Laurence Musgrove for establishing and maintaining this project, which provides community for poets and supports hunger relief through its sponsorship of Feeding Texas.

PROLOGUE: UNIFYING THEORY

When I learn an old lover is dead,
I feel a kind of stitching in my side,
invisible thread connecting form.

Past 80 now, I'm well beyond
ambitions and vain desires
like those that long ago split us apart,

the friction of two ideas of life
(disagreements, demands, concessions)
that all who ever loved know well.

She has been dead a score of years,
and the last time we spoke
I was barely a man. Every strand

of her life since then (family, career,
the better and worse, heart ache and heart's
joy) is matter dark to my knowing. Even so

I feel a string of light, a laser
threading us both, our hearts like beads,
joining me to her and her to me forever.

This same ray runs through everything
I ever loved and did not love. And oh!
How unbreakable it is! How hot! How bright!

OUT OF THE BLACKNESS ECSTATIC

Come forth into the light of things,
Let Nature be your teacher.

WILLIAM WORDSWORTH, "THE TABLES TURNED"
(*LYRICAL BALLADS*)

RAIN

What would be good for the next seven generations?

TRADITIONAL IROQUOIS WISDOM

That future that doesn't exist
is now. That forest, that fish,
that fawn of the fawn of the fawn
you didn't kill one foggy night
when you swerved on the road
as the pregnant doe
scampered away in the woods.

This is how you save tomorrow.
Watch out for herds on the shoulder,
and speak to the Little Ones with joy
that puts no price on the hours.
Make offerings of song and sun
to the Three Sisters and Four Winds.
Raise a good voice to Thunder.

Seven generations are risen in mist.
No one in the camps of your clan
recalls your name or deeds.
Yet all you did not do
or did rains in the now of that now,
filling the rivers,
refreshing the land.

A RECOLLECTION OF EVOLUTION IN SCUBA DIVING CLASS

When I breathed, my breath was lightning.

BLACK ELK, *BLACK ELK SPEAKS*

I drift at the bottom
of Broken Bow Lake,
below the thermocline
in the snow-globe stir of silt,
in the valveless night
of zero visibility.

Without mask or water lung,
without flipper or wetsuit,
my chest, my body—
breathless, bursting,
waiting, wanting—
holds the blood
at the rock edge
of consciousness,
abyss of drowning,
the chasm beyond
the buoy-marked limits
of circulation without oxygen.

Hearing the blindness
of the world's noise
muffled to a base note
of one decibel,
I remember
my airless beginning,
zygote certainty of mutation,
a billion years of transformation,

my eagerness for the sunny air,
for the sea-change gulp
of one deep breath
and the leaping into being
of some new fish
a million millennia
from this.

KALI

Grandmother rummaged
deep in her fat black purse
and pulled out a peppermint.

Untwisting the plastic
I learned very young that a spicy sweetness
comes out of the blackness

ecstatic,
a happy flapper dancing on the tongue
in the monsoon night of mouth,

a red and white wheel
like a rocket, like a starburst
sparking constellations in the tummy,

a brittle little skull
rolling its roundness
toward an understanding, arriving

long after we've hidden the wrapper
in a cool black pouch of earth.
Now I savor something sweet in her absence.

The flame of her magic,
shimmering, sizzling,
kindling the coolest jazz on my palate.

SECRET PLACE

Some days in my childhood
I needed for no one to find me.
Some of those days, I could slip
from the scene when I was dead,

raise the old door that covered the hole
in the brick foundation,
squirm under,
and shut it behind me.

Outside there were things to be done.
There were parents.
There were warnings
and expectations and big

brothers running about
killing, killing
zombies, headhunters, heretics,
outlaws, Indians, jerries and gooks.

They always killed me first,
the littlest one,
and in the thrill of their game,
paid me no mind when I was gone.

Under the house it was cool and still.
Bricks muffled the guns and grenades.
There were spiders and mice,
a dusty wood smell, darkness

spelled by slivers of light
passing though chinks in the brick.
There was watchful, watery peace
something like sleep.

9

WHEELS

When I was six
a caisson drawn
by six black horses
bore my grandpa
to his rainy burial.
Wheeling my garbage bin
out to the curb
today for some reason
I remember his memories
of trench and artillery
just as a young mother passes
pushing a stroller.

CALF

You shall go out leaping like calves from the stall.
MAL 4:2 (NRSV)

Chester stood at the fence in the morning
stroking the nose of a calf,
some agreement of animal energy connecting.

The boy who watched them, caring for both,
wondered about this world
where you love an animal you raise for slaughter.

All day the man and the boy hauled hay,
stacking the bales in Chester's barn.
The boy inhaled the dust and darkness.

Fresh-cut hay, animal dung.
The dry old barn with its own way of knowing,
storing up wisdom from fodder.

When they pitched the last bale
it was already dark.
Every inch itched, every muscle ached.

But he forgot his fatigue when Chester patted his arm:
Pup, that's a good day's work.
The boy leapt onto the bed of the flat-bed truck

for the ride home to supper.
The wheels raised dust on the River Road.
The boy inhaled the night, the pine and the water.

LIGHTNING

He is swimming alone
in the Mountain Fork River,
a boy at ease with night
and his nakedness in nature.
Rain begins to dapple
the face of the water.
He can hear the percussion
on trees and the river.
He can see up close the dance
and dissolve of splashes
ecstatic in the flashes.
He can feel on his head
the icy drumming,
ions of altitudes, high
to imagine, endless cycle
of going and coming.
He stays in the river.
In rain, in thunder,
in lightning, carried away
in a current he never expected.
Against good reason
of fatherly teaching,
he stays in the danger,
immersed in the power,
buoyant, alive,
now in the darkest dark,
now in light so dazzling.

LIVE ALIVE LIFE LIVED LIVES LIVING

for Elizabeth

In just a few days
my daughter will have
a son. Exhausted
by a walk up stairs,
heavy with life,
she looks out on winter
and awaits the solstice.
Expectancy brings her
a cup. Night is humming
to afternoon. She wonders
about the waning light,
recalling how once
when she was a girl
she teased a kitten
with a yellow string.
There was the rustle
of the live oak, a fly
on the screen, and bees
in the honeysuckle
outside her room.

ONE-HANDED TREE

for Sarah

The sun throws shadows into my bedroom
from the magnolia tree outside. If
what Plato said about the cave is true,
I am a shadow watching a shadow of a shadow.

Down the hall in her own room my daughter
is practicing yoga. The Cobra. The Crow.
The Cat and Cow. The Plow. I understand
there is even a pose called The Corpse.

I am chained in this cave by a sweet willingness.
As a boy, I dreamed of living alone in the woods.
I don't know how I already knew
how much it was going to hurt to love

so much the shades of this world. Over time,
with practice, you learn to hold still in
a thousand positions of loss. The expert can
impossible convolutions make seem natural

and relaxed. A little wind stirs outside,
and the shadow of a blossom begins to dance
on my blue comforter. I look out the window.
The petals of the flower are

as lithe and alive as my daughter's body.
The One-Handed Tree Pose, for stability
and strength. Destroyer of the Universe—hardest
of all—devoted to Shiva.

DOUBLE FEATURE

The most unfree souls go west, and shout of freedom.

D.H. LAWRENCE, *STUDIES IN CLASSIC AMERICAN
LITERATURE*

On Saturday afternoons
their mother dropped the brothers off
at the old Joy Theater.
Its ratty seats and sticky floors,
its dirty screen flickering in the dark
with silvery shades
of myth.

With popcorn and soda,
the boys consumed in utter joy
the thrill of how the west was won
and lost.

War paint, wagon trains, flaming arrows,
scalped settlers, injun-killing cowboys,
the brave Cavalry martyred on their horses,
gunfights and rough law,
whiskey, saloon girls,
greasy cards and derringers,
railroad tycoons, cattle barons, undertakers,
the town under siege, and always
the white-hatted rescue
of fledgling civilization—
its splintery boardwalk, its muddy street.

On Sunday mornings
the boys returned to the Joy,
rented for an hour
to a tiny flock of earnest Christians.

There kind, old Mrs. Rayburn
taught the boys to turn the other cheek,
to love their enemies,
to welcome persecution,
to heal the sick, cast out demons, raise the dead,
and above all else
to know
down to the rock bottom of their souls
that God is Love
and Love is All
in all.

THE RIVER OF
AFFIRMATION
AND JOY

The well-being of the EMT-Basic depends upon his ability to recognize that stressful traumatic situations do occur and the effect of those situations is felt by the patient, family members and the EMT-Basic. In recognizing this, the EMT-Basic must be aware of internal and external mechanisms to help himself, the patient, patient's families, EMT-Basic's family and other EMT-Basics deal with reactions to stress.

EMERGENCY MEDICAL TECHNICIAN-BASIC:
NATIONAL STANDARD CURRICULUM

BODHI

In a world that shreds
its avatars
your passion begins
on the third day

Holding a thorny twig
of myrrh
you stand in a circle
of fallen cerements
rejoicing and singing
yes yes yes here is the way

Though now you understand
the eagerness to die
you are eager
to return to the light

The bliss the darkness promises
can wait

You have so much to do
so much to say
when the stone is rolled away

ASHES

Her uncle killed her father, his brother,
when she was twelve. Now fire
has taken the rest—her brothers, sister, mother.
She stands in the charcoal ruins.
She is fourteen. Somehow she knows
they will sit at her table forever.
No future she can think of is worse.
Except for the one where they don't.

CRADLEBOARD

Almost twelve, fostered from age four.
Everyone knows she's not right.
Her nights have eyes.
She screams. She runs away.
She wears only black, not knowing it
the color of change.

Today with Mrs. Berry's class
she attends the past,
the Mayer Museum at Angelo State.
T-Rex, trilobites, raptor eggs, mammoth bones,
the wide-open jaws of megalodon
swallowing classmates six at a time.

Through ice, volcanoes, meteorites,
through epochs and eons,
she passes
with etherized indifference.
She sleepwalks into a room of color—
flocks of waterfowl dead and mounted,

crystal, silverware, amethyst vases,
walls and walls of paintings,
yet though she is fond of art
(her macabre ink drawings worry her therapist),
no vision in that whole bright hall
can enter her eyes.

Like a mouse in a maze,
she heads upstairs. Frontier days
are on display. Tack and saddles.
Wooden teeth. A chamber pot.
Medical tools—bone saw, scalpel, forceps.
A basin used by a prostitute.

Suddenly something calls to her—
an infant's cry,
which she alone can hear.
She stops, turns,
stands fossilized, staring down
at a Native American cradleboard.

Little more than a weathered plank
with rawhide bands
to hold the swaddled papoose.
Though frayed and soiled, the straps
that held it to a woman's back
still show a loving skill with beads.

The girl, transfixed, stares and stares,
gazes at that cedar board until she becomes
the baby there, searching
with her newborn eyes
a hundred years for Mother,
her mother

beaten, raped, forsaken, lost—
lost to war, to meth, to choices made—
woman's terror and woman's pain
living in her, bearing her
toward the blood
of motherhood.

The bus is loading.
Mrs. Berry seeks and finds
the girl still there, silent,
stoic as wood, apparently emotionless,
except for tears
streaking her stony face.

ESCAPING CHILDHOOD TRAUMA

   Fortunately
my father never shot
my mother and then turned
the gun around
and blew his own mind.
None of my brothers
lost their legs on the tracks
or got ripped like a
stud by
a band saw.
And my sister grew up
to marry an engineer
instead of being
strangled in puberty
and found
with her onyx eyes
open to the moon
in the woods beyond
Forrest Street.

   In fact
no one I held
in the grip of my need
got torn from the world
when I was a kid
except two
dogs, four cats,
and a litter of
kittens chewed
to bloody scraps
by a neighbor's pit
bull underneath our house.

One
of my friends
got his appendix out
and I got twelve
stitches in my knee
and a tetanus shot
from wrecking my new bike
at the dump.
But that's the worst.

I guess
you could say
I pretty well
escaped all
those soul-carving
lacerations
that shred
the very young,

unless you count
all the ones that cut
every night
on Walter Cronkite
while I sat
    cross
-legged on the floor
in front of the Tube
chewing
a chicken leg
or boiled potatoes
or soggy vegetables
trying

very hard

to swallow.

HAPPILY EVER AFTER

On his way to his wedding,
he came on the wreck—
two of his aunts, who'd left
for the chapel before him.

He stayed on the scene
until the jaws of life
chewed open the door
and ambulances ate the corpses.

When he got to the church,
there was blood on his shirt.
His bride, in her gown,
fell into him crying.

That was a wedding
where everyone cried.
And amid all the keening
for those two old maids,

still you could hear, I swear it,
like a descant swelling the grief,
bone-deep sobs of joy
for the happy couple.

FLAMES

Perhaps all the dragons in our lives are princesses who are only
waiting to see us act, just once, with beauty and courage.

Rainer Maria Rilke, *Letters to a Young Poet*

In the old myth of the dragon-slayer,
the dragon was no friend but heartless prohibition,
ferociously guarding a boon, a treasure.

We might call it transformation.
With so many dear friends doing battle with cancer,
of course I think these days of that fire-bellied beast.

The flames igniting their tissues,
singeing all the ropes and timbers of their bodies' lashings,
have burned away more than hair.

It seems their very being is perishing in fire.
What sword can I give my companions?
What charm can sing the dragon to sleep?

Deep in the furnace of my own fear,
how can I know the energy out of which it flows?
How can I welcome, take hold, and then let go?

Can I conjure a courage to unleash love?
Can I whisper "Death," "Mortality," "Nothingness"
and live in the blaze by which all things become?

When I come to the ruin of my own mythology,
will I scream in the inferno and curse its wings
or can I dance in the change and sing?

CHARITY

Toweling his groin in the locker room,
the lieutenant said, "A scrotum is a purse
for progeny." I'm not sure he heard
his own musing, but he's as likely as a drop
of sweat to fire off a metaphor,
so it fell on my ear like a barbell.

We're naked together five days a week.
I longed to reply in the zeitgeist
of the moment—if only I knew
what it was. Meanwhile
Flanagan (always cocked
and loaded) was quick
as the snap of a towel:
"That's a purse that isn't full
until everything in it is spent."

We all must do a lot of business
on our way to becoming human.
Even the heart (so near the privates
in the anatomy of men) hangs heavy
with the thrift of its transactions.
Like three sets of curls for our biceps
we expect some return on investment.

Let me offer an illustration
from Grandfather's pouch of stories.
In the old morality play, Everyman
bargains with Death
in the coinage of charity.
When he's abandoned by Goods,
Good Deeds seems pretty good company.

Once the lieutenant's jewels were dry
and he was again regulation
in his boots and desert fatigues,
he seemed the figure of valor and glory,
gung-ho to sack some city
with his co-ed contingent of Myrmidons.

For some reason, I remembered
my late friend Marsh,
an evolutionary biologist,
and how he was fond of saying,
"The philanthropist" (by which
he meant a good deed doer)
"is maximally selected against.
If you throw yourself on a hand grenade
you take your genes
right out of the gene pool."

Later that day I donate platelets.
A needle in my arm for two hours,
my feet up with *West Wing*,
is little to pay for what I mean to buy,
as if I could say what it is.

As I watch my red cells returning
to that hiding place of the spirit,
I know my friend is right.
Your purse can only be full
if it's empty. Of course
it doesn't make sense, but it's true.
Teach it to your progeny.

MAKING BREAD ON THE FOURTH OF JULY

Other seeds fell on good soil and brought forth grain, some a
hundredfold, some sixty, some thirty.

MATT 13:8 (NRSV)

In quarantine we all become bakers.
We go early to the store for yeast and flour.
We surf for tips and recipes.
We put a clean dry pall over the bowl
and wait for the dough to plumpen
like a healthy pregnant woman.

The leaven. The hot oven. The brown crust.
In the midst of plague
we are comforted.

When I slice the bread
the loaf suddenly opens
to a ploughed field in America's heartland.
I kneel and scoop a handful of earth.

The soil remembers melting glaciers,
receding oceans,
the unbroken sod of millennia,
wild horses lifting their faces to rain,
endless herds of stampeding bison,
nomadic tribes,
dog soldier, shaman, sweat lodge, ghost dance.

Lost now to the manifest greatness
of an ever-hungering nation.
Lost to the mule shoe and plough, to sturdy settlers.
Lost to the tractor and combine,

the prosperous, world-feeding farms
of the breadbasket.

I am a wandering child of the land.

Tasting all the loss
in a warm, buttered slice, I yearn
to stand in a golden field,
to touch with reverence the ripening grain
and believe in its hundredfold harvest.

SILENT

Whoever heard of night
using big words
to get what it wanted?
Star light comes to you
caroling, but there are
no words or music.

When you climb to the top,
you don't expect
the mountain to lecture.
Wind in an icy crevice
explains nothing that you think
needs explaining.

The tongues of flame that took
my father and mother
had nothing to say.
Because I was silent
and listened, I heard
the lesson and learned it.

THE RIVER OF AFFIRMATION AND JOY

for Ben

Because there is so little left of me,
I can hold it.
I can hold all the pain in the world.
I can hold this present darkness.

I can hold the tears of the little girl
whose father just won't love her.
I can hold the loneliness of a boy
who just can't find a friend.

I can hold the high school junior
who drove off the Wolf Creek bridge.
I can hold the college freshman, missing.
I can hold their broken families.

I can hold the unexpected diagnosis,
the prayers and pleading.
I can hold the empty chair
and Sunday visits to the cemetery.

I can hold the women held down,
the girls molested, bought and sold,
despair at the border, mules, meth labs,
cartels, coyotes, cages.

I can hold the man losing his breath
under the guilty knee of law.
I can hold the whole alphabet
of prejudice—age, class, ethnicity,

gender, race, religion, sex—all
the valves of our hearts clogged
with fear and rage down in
the fiery furnace of persecution.

I can hold spite and judgment,
shame and self-loathing—
ugliness, incompetence, rejection—
the bullets, pills, gas, razors, ropes.

I can hold the ruined seas and forests,
habitats fouled and paved,
species gone every day
from the breathing earth.

I can hold the deadly indifference
of nature—plague and parasite,
virus, venom, predator,
wind, water, rock, ice, fire.

I can hold the generations of war,
the slogans and demands
of ideology, revenge, ambition—
displacement, starvation, torture, graves.

I can hold the newborn baby unwanted.
I can hold the millions of abortions
and all the screaming polemics
in favor of life or choice.

I can hold the profiteer's greed and pride.
I can hold neglect and abuse of people and planet.
I can hold crime, imprisonment, injustice.
I can hold depression, addiction, madness.

I can hold the pathologies of faulty genes.
I can hold every presumption of brutality.
I can hold bruises, blood, and broken bones.
And I can hold my own impotence before the giant.

Slowly, over eons, the suffering of living things
erodes the softness—
soil and vegetation.
When this torrent grinds you down

to the rock bottom of your being
you can hold it.
You *must* hold it.
Hold it, and let it flow.

MOON IN A
MUDDY ARROYO

Wayfarer of the day, keep this in mind:
Lamp in hand, I traveled all night.
Summoned from the other shore
Adrift on my broken raft I sang my songs
As sere and withered leaves fell.

RABINDRANATH TAGORE, "KEEP THIS IN MIND"
(*LOVE SONGS*)

ERIS, MOTHER OF MANSLAUGHTER

There's something I couldn't see
When I was filled with hate.
Beautiful Eris blinded me.
I couldn't see you.

There's something I couldn't know
When I was thrilled with hate.
Beautiful Eris devoured me.
I couldn't know you.

There's something I couldn't have
When I was chilled with hate.
Beautiful Eris possessed me.
I couldn't have you.

Frozen, chewed, and blind with hate,
There's something I couldn't be.
Eris killed my heart and soul.
I couldn't be me.

NORTH AND SOUTH

This slavery breeds ugly passions in man.

HERMAN MELVILLE, *BENITO CERENO*

What a cute little jigaboo!
My father couldn't seem to help himself,
whenever he saw a black child searching
for lost balls beside Golf Lake, sipping
orange crush through a paper straw outside the A&P,
ambling the tracks that stretched to the part of town
where good white boys should never go.

Jigaboo, jigaboo.
He offered candy or coins from his pocket
like our legendary sea-roving great-grandfather
pulling beads and baubles from a sharkskin bag
to buy the friendship of the South Sea natives.
Displaced New England man, son of whalers,
with bright romantic notions of the noble savage,
my father thought the small black bodies
exotic, picturesque, and quaint.

He could never fathom my uncle's racist rage,
Uncle Jesse, bow-tie accountant,
married to my mother's baby sister
and kind as country milk in every other way.
Of course my father never knew him as a boy
among the poor white dogs of Caddo Parish,
dragonflies and shadows, water moccasins,
tarantulas, snapping turtles, the marsh and mud
of Caddo Lake. The bone of original sin,
whatever sin that is, lay buried deep in him, far out
of reach of Emerson, Bentham, or Beecher Stowe.

All his days its shadow ran him hard.
Frothing and howling through briery woods,
he chased the black beast in his brain,
fetching hate
at any sight or mention of the race:
nigguh nigguh nigguh.

It seasoned the barbecue we ate,
tainting the smoky meat, so tender
with the texture of his care.
It leeched into his hand-cranked lemon ice cream,
salting the shining sweetness of a summer day.

Our mother tried to teach us
to ignore his hate (*Don't be like that!*),
forgive him for it, and love him anyway.
After all he was our flesh and blood.

One Huck Finn Sunday he fished with us,
the scene along that sparkling bayou
like a Norman Rockwell idyll.
My uncle was content, amusing, tender
toward us, docile as the knob-kneed cypress
all the day, until late afternoon he saw them
picking their way along the shore toward us.

Two boys they were, easing
through the thick hot Southern air,
barefoot with nap hair, fishing net and poles,
and a mud cat string of keepers.
At the sight of them
I saw my Uncle Jesse clench
like a fist
around a rope,
and I was never so afraid.

Meanwhile, my father, lost
in some nor'easter reverie of Gloucester,
never noticed Uncle Jesse change.
When at last he looked up from his bobbing cork
and saw the boys, he shrieked with joy, *O look!*
Just lookit that now, lookit the cute little jigaboos.

SPIT

It was the year of love. It was the year of dreams.
It was the year of water cannons and Wallace for President.
It was the year Clyde and I
were the only boys in Journalism class.

The girls assigned us two to roam the school
in search of scoops. Most days we'd end up at
the Field House vending machines to split
a Coke or Nehi and laugh in the luck of our fantasies:
all those girls in our class, all to ourselves, all wanting us.

As we passed our bottle back and forth,
we named the ones we wished to kiss
until the final bell dismissed
all our delusions of sexual bliss.

One day one of us suddenly said, "Talk like this
could get us both lynched." All at once his blackness
opened up and let me in his unfinished history,
red with terror and with pain my skin
could never reckon or comprehend.

That news was a kind of anointing.
When we passed our chalice of purple soda
from his hand to mine, my hand to his,
our hands agreed to some unspoken covenant.

Neither of us wiped the spit.

Riots erupted in our school that year.
Lockers burned. Belts and fists.
Car windows shattered on the parking lot.
School dismissed.

Because we were friends, Clyde and I,
classmates cursed and spit on us.

All through the rage we stayed inside a faith
more intimate than a kiss—
daring, dangerous, deathless, deep,
streaming like the blood on our southern streets.

SAMARITAN

Ramon shoved his shotgun
down a gopher hole
and blasted.

"I don't know
if I got the son bitch
but I tried my damnedest."

Ramon turned 70
on the same summer day
I turned 65.

His tractor steers itself
by GPS.
Ramon, my second self.

"Put me on speed dial, bro,
in case you ever
drive your truck in the ditch."

As a young man
Ramón y su hermano
ran weed out of Mexico

on their motorcycles
"like those dudes
in *Easy Rider*."

About the same time
a girl in school
that I really liked

said that she couldn't go
out with me
porque soy gringo.

No sé
por qué lo menciono,
pero parece importante.

A FENCE GOT TIRED OF BEING A FENCE

A fence that kept these worlds apart
Decided just to up and move away.
I guess it got tired of keeping worlds apart,
So it just upped and moved away.

Have you seen what becomes of This and That,
What happens to Other when a fence removes?
When worlds that once were two are not,
The Now-One World is greater than two.

When there isn't anymore any more Over There,
There can't be any more Don't Come Here.
So everywhere the wind blows through
Is Hallowed Ground—One Ground, not two.

Thanks to the fence that moved away
The two old worlds are One and New.
It shows us all we ask a fence to do:

Keep them out and keep us in.
Keep the good things in for us.
Keep the bad things out for them.

Consider what could be—and should—
If all the fences woke up one day
And saw they weren't doing any good,
So they just upped and moved away.

HILLEL

The rabbi asked:	*What is the point and purpose of Holocaust Studies?*
The talmidim replied:	Never again.
The rabbi asked:	*How?*
The talmidim replied:	Next year in Jerusalem.
The rabbi asked:	*Is there no gas in the City of Peace?*
The talmidim replied:	Yes, there is plenty.
The rabbi asked:	*What would induce you to use it against your enemies?*
The talmidim were silent.	They could not reply.
The rabbi asked:	*What is the point and purpose of Holocaust Studies?*

EVERY BEAUTIFUL NAME

And when you take your next breath as we enter the fifth world
There will be no *X*, no guidebook with words you can carry.

JOY HARJO, "A MAP TO THE NEXT WORLD"
(*HOW WE BECAME HUMAN*)

When I browse the names on the Virtual Wall, I'm surprised how
many begin with Q. I expected a galaxy of As and Bs—Aadland
to Byus might take an hour to read. Even the Zs are prolific.

There is only one X, though: 1LT Augusto Maria Xavier. A page
to himself. Lonely as a castaway. Rare as a mark on a treasure
map. As if a fragment of All can be less than the whole.

If you click on his name, you learn that Augusto flew an A-4C
SKYHAWK and died while providing close air support.

"His body was never recovered."

I won't try to explain my penchant for names.

Sometimes I get out the old phone book and read a column at
random with bardic reverence like the glossary of the Mahab-
harat or a Homeric catalogue of captains, ancestors, ghosts.

I like it best when the people are real—by which I mean they re-
ally lived one time or are living now. Or someday will.

I scan the death notices and birth announcements in my local
newspaper, sounding the names as a blessing.

Perusing those online sites of best baby names, I like to imagine
new-born Olivia or Liam.

I can't help but imagine little Emma or Ava, Oliver or Noah when they get to the age that I am now.

A life should repay a mother's labor at least. So I imagine Augusto Maria Xavier meeting me for coffee in the Dairy Queen. He would be 80 this year.

Would he talk about Nam? Would I tell him my lottery number and explain why I didn't enlist?

Would I ask him about his middle name? "Why not Mario or Marius? Were you named for the Virgin? Or the Roman god of war?"

Augusto never answers me.

I live a long way from Vietnam, where his body came apart, but if what I read somewhere is true, some of his atoms are in me now.

My youngest child's second child is due in a month. She will get some of his atoms, too.

Her name is Eleanor Grace, which I like very much.

I helped to choose her mother's name, Elizabeth, and the names of another daughter and my son, Sarah and Benjamin. Well, the names came to my wife, like gung-ho volunteers, but I approved.

I still like these classic Old Testament names, although more and more the book itself repulses and terrifies, with all its news of exile, chosenness, judgment, genocide, apocalypse.

Well, all the old epics are written in blood, and some is good news.

The Mahabharat has hundreds of proper names. Long lists of allies and enemies. Arjuna himself has 14 different names, including one which means "scorcher of foes."

According to one list of *least popular* names I found online, the rarest of given names is Pax, which isn't surprising.

It makes me wonder how much the names we give our children help to determine who they turn out to be.

Sometimes it seems like people live into their names, as if David or Peter or Dawn or Lolita could itself be a kind of destiny.

I wish I could name some baby boy or girl Pax (it's a unisex name) and see what happens.

People call God by a lot of different names. We can't seem to help it, though it might be better if we refrained.

Shiva, Jehovah, Wakonda, Zeus, Allah, the Dao. A thousand and one epithets. But I guess the Ineffable is still the Ineffable. Absolute is Absolute.

All the difference must be somehow somewhere in us who do the naming and use the names.

Allah has 99 names. The one I like best is *al Waahid*.

I looked for this name on the Virtual Wall. While I was looking I decided for no reason at all to count the Ws, but I couldn't pass Walker without losing count.

So many Walkers!

There are 70 panels East and 70 West, tens of thousands of names, arranged by date of casualty, but *Waahid*, my favorite of the 99 names for Allah, is nowhere engraved in the granite.

Can you find Pax?

I know the answer. The question is for you. Everyone should read all those names at least once a year. The President and every member of Congress should have to read them all aloud like an oath before taking office.

And there are plenty of other names from plenty of other wars. They should read them, too—all our own soldiers, of course, but also allies, civilians, and even the "hostiles"—hosts of them killed in a host of wars.

There should be a Vietnam War Memorial that includes all the names together, U.S. troops, U.S. allies, the Vietnamese, both South and North, Chinese, Cambodians, Laotians—more than three and a half million in all.

Augusto is the very first name on panel 6E, right next to John R. Cowan and directly above Kenneth A. Bodell. I hope they enjoy one another's company.

Their atoms are mixing—if what I read somewhere is true.

Most people can grieve for a fallen comrade, a parent, a child, or even a pet. But what about the enemy?

Grief is nothing less or more than a sense of diminishment in homage of life.

Tat Tvam Asi, it says in the Upanishads.

This means "You are that."

Atman is Brahman.

Which means you and I are in essence one with God or Ultimate Reality (whatever name you prefer) and so with each other.

Which means we are one as well with Augusto and Kenneth and John, and one with all they killed in Vietnam, with all who died in every war.

And so also with Olivia and Liam, Ella and Lizzy.

Can you believe this?

I don't know if I can.

But I guess if God ever needs another name, any of these will do fine.

BREAD

De Lord God ob heaven be praise', I got my own ag'in!

MARK TWAIN, "A TRUE STORY, REPEATED WORD
FOR WORD AS I HEARD IT"

The flesh of her suffering
is the bread she was baking—
biscuits in an iron skillet—
body of all she has lost.

It falls from her hand
as she welcomes again the homeless
child of her blackness,
born into slavery. Love

she refused to abandon
has called him back to her kitchen
with a voice from the fire.
The battles they fought

have left them both bloody,
but now her alto of laughter
holds the full measure of weeping
in a trumpet of joy.

The boy comes to her hungry.
She takes some of her bread
from the floor. Breaks it for him.
Smothers it with butter and honey.

CROSSROADS

Stand at the crossroads, and look . . .

JER 6:16 (NRSV)

When you flee the thing
you do not want to be, look
for a trail that crosses the highway
before the fork to Daulis

and Thebes. You must slow down
to see an opening in the forest.
In the shade of Parnassus, stop.
Leave your car to the winds

of onrushing traffic. Like water
in a low place, enter the woods
under dogwood branches.

Without scout or guide,
on four legs or two or three, seek
a path too narrow for kings.

WASP MAN, OR BODIES OF PROTEST AND JUSTICE

for those, like me, who have a white, male body in America

There's a way out of this mess, and it requires each of us to begin
with our own body.

RESMAA MENAKEM, *MY GRANDMOTHER'S HANDS*

I.

On many sides the sunny walls of my house are warm to my
  neighbors.
On many sides my windows let in a vision of flowers and trees,
  butterflies and birds.
My curtains part to invite the four winds on many sides.
My teeth stand watch over my words on many sides.
My fingers unfurl gestures of generosity on many sides.
The moon orbits the garden on many sides and for once I see its
  many faces.
The shore embraces the lake on many sides and the boats go
  sailing.
Feathers adorn the mockingbird and fur the lion on many sides.
Sound serenades the singer, night caresses lovers on many sides.
On many sides the grave swaddles the coffin cool with the dark.

II.

O Wasp Man, Proud Man, latest second coming of the emperor,
  listen.
Like you I've spent my life pale as a ghost in transparent suprem-
  acy haunting the rotting citadel of America.

Like you I've lived my whole life jerking the joysticks of the
    American dream and creed.
Like you I've spent my life contriving many myths to deny my
    systemic advantages.
Like you I've spent my life building churches and country clubs
    just for us.
Like you I've celebrated with pig meat and fireworks the inven-
    tory of manifest destiny.
Like you I've conscripted subalterns to paint the three boats of
    Columbus and tar all the wood and riggings of the Middle
    Passage.
Like you I've sung the subtext of lynching.
Like you I've had a good laugh at the rape joke.
Like you I've made all the laws then assembled the posse for
    whiskey.
Like you I've known I could get away with all I could get away
    with.

Now you have shown me the fault lines of my attitudes.
You have drilled too deep into my comatose conscience, and the
    crude of actual history finally gushes from the darkness of the
    brain's deepest strata.
You have worn out all the lies we have used to excuse our toxic
    identity.
Now I am hoping there is something like reincarnation.
I am hoping for a second chance for our caste.

III.

In my next life I want me some dreadlocks.
In my next life I want my skin mahogany or olive.
In my next life I want a nose as broad and proud as Africa so I
    can smell your fear in the jungle.
In my next life I want to join Pussy Riot and bang my ax on the
    jail doors.

In my next life I want spiked heels to walk over your greenback
   patriarchy.
In my next life I want to shout through a silver beard *bismillah*
   five times a day on the Porch of Deplorable.
In my next life I want to show you the edge of my knife and the
   many shades of hair on my lodge pole.
In my next life I want epicanthic folds in my eyes and no tears for
   your inferior SAT scores.

I want to pull all the nails from your house so you have to build
   anew on the vacant lot of apartheid.
I want to push your pillars apart and laugh in the rubble.
I want to perform my ablutions in your heritage.
I want to steal the grievances you feed your kids and replace them
   with Sufi parables.
I want to wear my best halal to your barbecue.
I want to cremate all your unkosher hot dogs and pork chops
   under a crescent moon with the Star of David.
I want to pass a Bill of Rights for every avatar that you have de-
   nied, even Jesus.
I want an Amendment that you can only make beer from the
   unfiltered taps of Detroit and Jackson.
I want to cap the phallic spigots of dark money so you cannot
   breed swastikas.
I want to return as your great physician to inoculate your sick
   blood with a pride parade.
I want to remove your chronic orientalism and transplant jas-
   mine and lotus.
I want to be the witch you can't resist and liberate your better
   angels with herbs from the highest mountain.
I want to spit in your eggs just because you can't see me.
I want to force feed you the nuts and seeds of your unsolicited
   groping.
I want to beat my aboriginal drum in your pigment.
I want to tell you there's simply no cure.

I want to stand my ground in a black hoodie at your cocktail
    party and you with no AR-15.
I want to make you confess to your porn stash on *The 700 Club*.
I want to conceive justice and you're certainly not the father.
I want to abort your sterile idea of equality.
I want to force you to marry your rapist.
I want to force you to have the baby.
I want to pour sand in the oil of your Crusade.
I want to bash all the rotors of your Islamophobia.
I want to wear a hijab to the funeral of your misconceptions.
I want to teach your favorite dog to say *black lives matter*.
I want to raise up Golgotha in place of your gun safe.
I want to answer your urgent call in Hindi.
I want to burn fossil fuels in your bed with the ooze and odor of
    Sulphur River.
I want to tear the curtain in two in the drug store when you go
    for erectile dysfunction.
I want to feed all your pie to the poor in spirit.
I want to close every bar just as you park your pickup.
I want to catch you at night in my speed trap like an arrow in
    your recreation.
I want to rip away your delusions like intimate waxing.
I want to offer you the mercy of pirates.
I want to make sure you see it coming.

In the hope that you might wake up.
In the hope that you might be transformed.
In the hope that you might ask forgiveness.
In the hope that it might set you free.
In the hope that you might become human.

IV.

O Wasp Man, Proud Man, may there be a second chance for our
    caste.
In my next life I am all that our kind is afraid of.

In my next life I am your shadow, I project all your archetypes of
the darkness within you.
In my next life I cast off the limits of race like the chains of a
slave.
In my next life I cast off assumptions of gender like the cords of
your commandments.
In my next life I pare away your lust and violence with the pure
diamond of meditation.
In my next life I wash away your ignorance and fear with crystal
waters of the Dao.
In my next life I wind my way among continents loving and
becoming in the joy of awakening, in the ecstasy of salvation, in
the bliss of freedom you refused ever to give or imagine.

V.

Be quiet.
Listen.
Feel your denial of the suffering body.

Hear wind in the sails carrying *you* from *your* native continent.
Hear *your* blood and bones being auctioned.
Turn *your* back to the slaver's lash
and hear the scraping of *your* feet on the ground,
your skin slicing open.

Be quiet.
Listen.
Feel your denial of the battered body.

Recoil at the sudden shock of violence.
Hide *your* cuts and bruises and pretend it's *your* fault.
Try desperately to hold onto *yourself*
when no one believes *you*
and *your* only option seems to be more of the same.

Be quiet.
Listen.
Feel your denial of the starving body.

Hear the pleading of *your* hungry children.
Hear poverty choking on every morsel *you* swallow.
Swim through razor wire on the border
and hear the charges against *you* shouted by fist-shaking mobs
in a language *you* can't understand.

Be quiet.
Listen.
Feel your denial of the voiceless body.

Hear police storming *your* ghetto.
Hear iron wheels carry *you* to prison.
Strip off *your* clothing
and pace bare-footed on the floor of *your* cell—
lynch mob, electric chair, gas chamber, gallows.

Be quiet.
Listen.
Feel your denial of the dying body.

Feel a knee on *your* throat and hear *yourself* not breathing.
Hear the coroner's scalpel open *your* chest.
Take a good look in *your* heart,
and hear the pain of twenty generations.
Let the sobbing and screaming make *you* keen for change.

VI.

Wadea Al-Fayoume I love and become you in the holiest of holy
    nights as you walk into Paradise at the feet of your mother.

Breonna Taylor I love and become you in a screaming ambulance as you answer every call of disaster.

George Floyd I love and become you in the buzzing heat of summer and you keep on breathing for all the world.

Heather Heyer I love and become you in the street and you keep on directing traffic.

Eric Garner I love and become you on the pavement and you keep on tending the parks and gardens of the dream.

Tamir Rice I love and become you in all the art you might have created.

Martin King I love and become you on the balcony and you keep on preaching your shining imperishable from the steps of Lincoln.

Joseph Gelders I love and become you in the fundamental laws of the stars and you keep on teaching the ten words from the angel of truth.

Matt Shepherd I love and become you tied to a fence and you keep on blessing the stars of Wyoming.

Mercedes Williamson I love and become you under the changing leaves of Rocky Creek and you keep on making everyone beautiful who wants to be beautiful.

Jesse Washington I love and become you on the steps of City Hall and you keep illuminating the harvest with your burning body.

Mickey Schwerner I love and become you, Andrew Goodman I love and become you, James Chaney I love and become you in

the flashing lights of Jim Crow and you keep on building the
temple.

Manuel Moralez, Román Nieves, Longino Flores, Alberto García,
Eutimio Gonzales, Macedonio Huertas, Tiburcio Jaques, Am-
brosio Hernández, Antonio Castanedo, Pedro Herrera, Viviano
Herrera, Severiano Herrera, Pedro Jiménez, Serapio Jiménez,
Juan Jiménez I love and become you beneath the breathless
moon of Presidio County where the Mystery sings with you
in the integrity of silence denying every border and wall of the
heart.

VII.

Named and unnamed, known or forgotten, I put my hands in
    your wounds and we know the tangible truth of suffering.
I love and become you and we cry for all the blood in the aspira-
    tion of heaven.
I love and become you and we cry for self-denying and self-
    creating love.
I love and become you and we need no words to cry.
We cry with the fearless, deathless voice of perpetual oneness.
We cry *victory now!*
And we cry *yes!* to the beauty of every body.
And we cry *hope is the transfiguration of ignorance!*
And we cry *empathy is the epiphany of all our pain!*
And we cry *a tomb can never contain tomorrow!*
And we cry *the now that we need is always in our hands!*
And we cry *the abundance of life is everlastingly within our reach!*
And we cry *freedom for everyone not a minute to waste!*
And we cry *justice!*
And we cry *equality!*
And we cry *sister and brother!*
And we cry!
We cry!
We cry!

ENCHANTED ROCK

Like eagle that Sunday morning
Over Salt River. Circled in the blue sky
In wind, swept our hearts clean
With sacred wings.

JOY HARJO, "EAGLE POEM" (*IN MAD LOVE AND WAR*)

CANYON'S COUNSEL

I know how sky welcomes moon,
how moon adorns lake with light,
how lake enlarges to let river in,
how river carves canyon,
how canyon takes counsel with sky,
asking, *What do I do with this abyss*
created by the grit of my own erosion?
Infinite and eternal sky replies to canyon,
First praise the space that river has opened,
then find something bright
arising in the night inside you,
and bid it welcome.

MANDALA

The center of the Mandala is the Now-moment, where, through the
quality of attention, we constantly create ourselves anew.

RICHARD MOSS, *THE MANDALA OF BEING*

Here
　　　　on my red brick patio
　　　　　　a couple of

　　　　　　yellow and green
　　　　striped lizards are
playing,

exploring
　　　　the cracks and crevices,
　　　　　　　darting from sun

　　　　　　　to shadow, from shadow
　　　　to sun,
diverging,

converging,
　　　　scrawling
　　　　　　　invisible lines—

　　　　　　　triangles,
　　　　swirls,
parabolas—

to trace a crazy
　　　　mandala.
　　　　　　　Now

                    I know how it is
            possible
to live

joyfully in this world
        without rockets
                    or roads.

HEADWATERS

In all the years I lived
in San Marcos I never went
to Aquarena Springs
to see the famous swimming pig
or to watch the mermaids
picnic in the crystal water.
But often on summer Saturdays
I snorkeled below the falls,
headwaters of the San Marcos River.

Up from the Edwards Aquifer
through two thousand springs,
the water defines clarity.
Don't get trapped under the falls,
they warned me,
but the pressure and the motion
pushes away all trace of sediment
to carve a bright fantastic world
of stone washed by eons.

Sometimes I let the river wash
my porcine flesh
like a lazy fish downstream
and I would drift and swim
in a slow and shady pool,
fanning the wild rice with my flippers
and peeping into crevices
along the shore with an eye out for
the Texas blind salamander.

Really I was myself
just a little creature made of water
and dust, awash with delight

in the deepest, purest love of earth,
seeing
at that moment
everything there was to see around me
and nothing at all behind me
or ahead.

ECOLOGUE

for Mom

I saw a cardinal in a jar, nowhere
near where any jar should be. The jar
stood upright on the ground without a lid
except the air, but though he hopped
and beat his wings against the glass,
the cardinal could not rise.

He sang a warning to the woods.
I scanned the trees for mate and nest
but saw no fluttering among the leaves
and heard no signal of distress.

A jar can be a useful thing,
but this was like a well, a pit
he'd fallen in. A tomb, and he
was some poor Lazarus or Christ
who'd come alive inside his grave
with no messiah to call him forth,
without a god to roll the door.

What accident or impulse put him there?
What band of brothers jealous of his coat?

Did he see a cat gone feral far
away from town and jump inside
in fear of claws and teeth? After all
some people, with their bigger brains,
have leapt into a refuge that became a keep.

More plausibly he spied a seed
or chased a bug, unaware

that there is such a thing as glass,
solid, but invisible as air.

Unaware? Who leaves a jar
out in the wilderness, and why?
I hope whoever placed it there
forgot or lost it and did not
intend to trap a living thing
so gorgeously essential to the world.

> *A self asleep conceives*
> *the cruel or careless act.*

Startled by those words, which came
to me as if the bird had spoken them,
I backed away. I listened.
I watched the cardinal watching me.

The sky and forest seemed to gather all
around the jar, and it became
umbilicus of earth, and he,
the bird, the unborn heart of everything,
the wild, red life always eager to arise.

> *The self awake bears*
> *every kind and caring deed.*

Kneeling there,
I gently, very gently, tipped the jar.
Its lid of air became an open door.

HORSE HORSES HORSEMAN

Seven red horses are galloping
north through a dry ravine.
I'm not at all sure I'm happy to see them.

Millions of people are massing
in all the world's capitals,
shaking their fists at power.
Shouldn't I be there with them
astride a white stallion named Justice?

I would much rather follow
seven red horses
as they leave the ravine
cutting west over boundless grasslands
that have never known sickle or mower.

Mobs know all about blades,
the sharper the better.
You can hear the angry speeches
keen as fangs of lightning.

Seven red horses started running
because one of them dreamed
of corral and cattle drive,
cavalry and cannon.

You can hear the scream of their power
in the thunder of hooves on the prairie.

Lightning strikes in the desert.
Suddenly I am galloping
over oceans of grasses
in the tracks of seven horses.

I know where they are heading,
up the slope of the continent,
away to the highest divide,
far from every sword and saddle.

NOMAD

They claim this mother of ours, the Earth, for their own use, and
fence their neighbors away from her, and deface her with their
buildings and their refuse.

SITTING BULL, *SITTING BULL'S MESSAGE FROM SPIRIT LIFE*

While making the rounds of the world,
Craving came to my door begging refuge.
She was enticing, exciting, and gratifyingly needy.
I loved her madly. For a while I was happy.

She soon became greedy and began to take over
my life with her Amazon Prime and Pay Pal.
Almost dead from overindulgence, I roused
my Craving for a hike in the Big Thicket.

At an old hunting camp we encountered a nomad,
one of the ancients buried with the seasons.
I thought it would be nice to learn to walk
through the forest without making footprints.

Immediately my Craving demanded lumber,
rubber tires, and a bouquet of rare orchids.
What can you say to pine and palmetto,
what excuse can you make to jaguar and heron,

what machines can you show a vanished people
to warrant the theft of their land and living?
The Ishak guided us down a shadowy track
to where it met a path forking off to a different future.

In that future, oil was never discovered.
I wanted to go, but my Craving resisted.
The trail we were on, not really a trail
but an overgrown jungle, kept going and going.

I knew it would take me all the way back
to Mesoamerica before the Santa María.
I wanted to go, but my Craving resisted.
So we returned to the city and take-out for dinner.

Things were never the same between us,
now that I knew how little you need a lot.
Craving grew sickly, thin as a tapeworm.
She left me in the winter for another lover.

AARON

The wood we gathered
in the afternoon
tells its story
as it burns: change
from seedling to sapling,
from branch to fuel.
Its theme is falling.
Somehow it becomes
the flames, and the flames
point the way.
I too first came
to this place as a boy.
Same abandoned
look-out tower.
Same patch
of berries, once
again in bloom.
From where I sit
I see
two decades' growth
has changed the view,
though not so much
you'd notice it
unless you wanted to.
To my son
it is all very new,
this night out
in the wilderness,
this mountain reverence.
I want to sit
across the fire
and look
until he sees

me sitting where he sits
vested
in the same fiery light.

JUVENILE

You spot the bird hiding under the flame acanthus.
A juvenile, unable to fly. You know how small
its chances are. What can you do?

For days it hides between the bushes and the fence.
Acanthus, hawthorn, roses bloom.
All nature seems alive and young.

You watch its mother bring this beggar food and chase away
the neighbor's cat. Every day you think you'll see
its tell-tale feathers on the grass.
Suddenly it flies.

Across the earth, slaughter is necessity and sport.
Insects, animals, people die. Innocents die. *How long, O Lord,
how long?* What can you do?

Rejoice for the rise of a single bird.
Rejoice for dangerous and determined love.
Rejoice for joy that sings in sanctuaries where sorrow was.

ISLE

I shall wear white flannel trousers, and walk upon the beach.

T.S. Eliot, "The Love Song of J. Alfred Prufrock"

When I became unfrocked, I cast away
commandments with all my priestly garments
and found a haven in the tropics, a hut
between sand and sky, the sea and forest.

Here nobody wants to dress in black.
There is no one to give my collar.
Soothed by the soft sea breeze, I wear
white linen trousers that fit me like a vapor.

With watercolors and impressions,
I paint my friendly neighbors, hills and ocean.
The tides are teaching me how to be
at peace with coming and going.

Just now, a jet is passing out on the horizon.
Its bending contrail threads the cumulus,
already vanishing, impermanent as I,
and vested in the beatitude of morning.

SHAMANIC

In my vision I saw myself on the central mountain of the world.
BLACK ELK, *BLACK ELK SPEAKS*

On the peak
of Enchanted Rock.
No doors.
No windows.

Day or night.

Wind
from all directions.
Voices
from all directions.

Brothers, sisters,
daughters, sons,
listen.

With love in your hearts
for all you see
listen.

Nothing
is closed to you.

Here is the center
from which you can see
everywhere

the center.

All around you a circle
of circles
of infinite radius.

Here you laugh
at the door people.
Here you laugh
at dreams of stasis.

My children,
you will encounter
many strange things
on the earth.

If ever someone
standing on a threshold
says to you
"This is the only door"
go away
at once.

Day or night.

Go.
Climb
some Enchanted Rock.

THE ORDEAL
OF MARRIAGE

Marriage, as I said, is not a love affair; it is an ordeal.

JOSEPH CAMPBELL, *THOU ART THAT*

STAR AND DITCH

Woe! By the very boundaries of Night
Orpheus his Eurydice
Saw, lost, and killed.

BOETHIUS, *THE CONSOLATION OF PHILOSOPHY*

What love is this that charms
the Dog of Hell? Infamous Furies
and the Lord of Death himself
are overborne.

Your little wick of human will
in mad descent to the deepest pit
has sparked from the conflagration of the heart
a Calliope spell.

Now seize for once and all
the radiance of your song.

You did not come with your lyre
to light the dark for a rotten corpse.
Take the living lady by the hand, and leave
the night dawning down below.

Listen! O listen as you go!
Hear the harmony of star and ditch
and tune your eyes to sing
the crystal vision in your pain.

The highest octave of the light
is in your range.

PLAY MATES

Because we were the youngest two
of all the troop of kids on Taylor Street
the big kids married us.
Angelina was three or maybe four.
I was just a little more.

It was a summer eve. They must've been bored.
Angelina and me, we had no say.
The church was in the alley where we played.
The birds and bees were literal.
Our altar was a garbage can.

Angelina stood beside me looking scared.
I leaned to her and whispered,
"I won't hit you."
Like your daddy hits your mom is what I meant.
She knew and smiled.

The next day, Angelina had a baby,
like they always do.
She delivered in the Adams's garage,
among the boxes, rags, and oily tools.
The baby was her baby doll, a ragged, ratty, dirty thing.

They laid Angelina on the floor,
pulled her skirt up,
pulled her panties off,
and, pointing, said to me,
"The baby comes from there."

I stared, of course, incredulous,
then looked in Angelina's big, dark eyes.
I saw in them

what I had never seen before,
have not seen since.

The labor took
just a minute or two.
When they were through, they said
I was the luckiest, happiest husband,
I was the proudest dad.

THE WHEEL OF MAYA

This grackle is the sovereign of his passions.
Behind the ER, perched above the dumpster,
he explains the afternoon to an acorn.

Meanwhile, Tia Gabriela has left
the tortilla on the griddle a little too long,
branding the bread with an icon of the Virgin.

Tio Matias sends the scorched Lady whirling
like the Milky Way toward the kitchen wall.
His plate of frijoles follows, also spinning.

Then with the momentum of a comet
his fist darkens the cheek of mi tia.
At the Icehouse, his usual stool is waiting

for his wrath to rub its roundness on the bar,
already polished by indignities
through eons of centrifugal motion.

Out on the blue Atlantic, heat
is lifting moisture from the swelling ocean
above the wreckage of some lost armada.

A satellite watches the hurricane forming,
saying: "Puerto Rico, Cuba, Florida, get ready.
This is your warning."

HARRISON, ARKANSAS

Ay, you shall be together even in the silent memory of God.

Khalil Gibran, "On Marriage" (*The Prophet*)

We got married in the morning and drove
two hours up Highway 7 to Harrison, Arkansas.

At our hotel too soon, we drifted downtown, in and out
of shops, side by side, just beginning to glue

our bodies together. We bought red Converse All Stars
with the fee that Father Shoemaker refused.

Your mother sang in his choir.
He consoled you when your father died.

We sat in his office for hours learning to live
as one flesh until one of us dies.

Why were we there in Harrison, Arkansas,
on the first day of our covenant?

Years before in that same town, your grandfather
faced a mob of vigilantes to protect his young family

then escaped in the night in a hurry
with murderous men at his heels.

Passing the first night of our future in Harrison,
Arkansas, had nothing to do with the past.

It was just on the way to where we wanted to be
on the way to where we were going.

Nevertheless, walking back to our hotel
with a shoebox under my arm

I saw your grandfather driving his wagon
through town in the middle of a strike.

He held the reins like a delicate ribbon, as if afraid
that gripping too tightly might break them.

With only a look I assured him
and just at that moment you took my hand.

Nothing needs to be forever
to be worth keeping.

For years we wore those red canvas high tops.
Today I still see them

and our long dead officiant, Father Shoemaker,
returning our check without saying a word.

ARACHNID

Consciousness is one of the great mysteries of science—perhaps the greatest mystery.

Graham Hancock, "The Consciousness Revolution"

A machine is breathing for our son.
He eats through a tube in his belly.
He has entered a room, seedless and deep,
where the cord of nature is severed.

My love, you must climb a spider's thread
to the North Star. I will be the mountain
where he walks and you the light to kiss his face.
We can watch him grow to manhood.

We will cheer as he passes every trial, slays
the tyrant and wins the beautiful maiden.
Then drop from the stars, arachnid,
return, and hold me again with all your arms.

A SMALL BLUE FLAME

In the middle of the thunderstorm my plumber calls
me from across the street to tell me
Half your roof is gone. Yeah I said I heard it go
and wondered to myself What do you do
in the middle of a storm when your plumber calls
to tell you half your roof is gone?

Isn't it obvious? I ask myself. You fall
in love with something. Quick. Maybe
with the small force of the blue flame
that lights the hot water heater whenever
the hot water heater needs lighting.
Or with the mouse you can barely hear
still scratching in the wall over the noise
of your house dying violently.

Really almost anything will do.

    For a year once
I admired a girl on the same bus.
I was a rodent scratching on the wall
of adolescence, too much a mouse to love her.
My mind kept telling me No, my little human ego,
weak as a wisp of straw in the wind,
forbidding me with thunderous arguments
the F5 blow of her rebuff.
She was too flawless, too rare, too beautiful
up there, two grades above me
in the striations of the supercell.
So I stopped myself from falling.
Hard as a chunk of ice hitting the earth,
I stopped myself.

But why should I stop now, I ask,
now with the storm raging,
now that a hostile wind
is fighting with lumber and nails to carry me
in pieces to a different state?

I guess you wonder if it's possible
to fall in love with something, anything,
inside a thunderstorm.
A girl, a mouse, a flame. Maybe even
(strangest thing) perhaps your wife,
an object these many years,
now calmly comforting your fetal children
while junk from thirty counties
beats against the walls at a hundred miles an hour.

Well, I promise I will tell you, if I make it through
in more or less one piece.
I'll tell if it is possible
to fall in love with something quick
inside a storm.
I'll tell you how I cowered on the floor in the hall
of my shuddering house and did
for once
or did not do
what I could never do.

RUTH

Lighting our table
the flame of a single candle
still as the stroke of *alif*.

Who would guess in this combustion
the violence of a million molecules
fueling the stasis?

The bread she offers,
gleaned from an alien harvest,
bears the flavor of ripened sunlight.

Later, when she lies in my arms
curved and small as *yod*,
with the soft glow of a candle,

I know I am
holding the power of all the galaxies,
the light of the first word spoken.

PROVISION

Of all in this realm of particles and force
nothing is mine.

Not the beans or bread on my plate.
Not the tea in my glass.
Not "my" plate or "my" glass.
Not the woman who cooks and bakes and sets the table.
Not the song that she sings as she lights a candle.

Consider the bowl of the body.
The blood, made in the bones, enters and leaves the heart
like a modest allowance.
Can I own a single cell?
Can I save a breath for a rainy day?
Can I earn interest on a swallow?

As we sit together, the woman and I, light spreads over the table
and over our faces.
But the light and the flame are no more mine
than they are the candle's.

The hand that butters the bread is not mine.
The teeth that chew are not mine.
The tongue that tastes is not mine.
The stomach is not mine.

Neither is any thought mine nor the will to love.

Still, holding her hand and mumbling in the mystery,
I offer thanks (thanks that is not mine)
to the nothing whose we are
for the bounteous marrow of this poverty.

WE WENT FOR A DRIVE

Without words, without even understanding
lovers find each other.

ADAPTED FROM LAO TZU, *TAO TE CHING*

She said, "Come for a drive with me, come
while the earth is in bloom.
We'll see waves of wild plum on hillside seas
and lightning on the lake in the late afternoon."

She said, "Come to a movie with me, come
sit in the flicker of comedy.
We'll see a chance kiss, hearts given away,
turns and twists, and a happy finale."

She said, "Come to the dance with me, come
to a phonic sensation.
We'll see joy twist her hips, grace walk on the moon,
and love beckon with vogue undulation."

She said, "Come to the farm with me, come
where soil is tilled and sewn.
We'll see colts in the meadow, chicks in down suits,
and a new moon held in the arms of the old."

She said, "Come into my dream with me, come
to my candle's rays.
We'll see children running through all the seasons
and fire in the hearth at the close of our days."

She said, "Come share your life with me, come
let me be your only one."
And as all we would never be slept on in the night,
all that we ever would rose with the sun.

It was easy to give her my life, easy
as a school-boy day in June.
She said, "Come for a drive with me, come."
What better to do on a young afternoon?

PHONE

It was April when she called you.
There was fighting outside your dorm room.
"Hold it down," you said.
"Hey, guys, please hold it down."

The stuffy phone booth in the lobby.
Crude drawings and graffiti.
With your ear to the receiver,
you leapt into the spell
of her unexpected invitation.

Squatting in the coffin of that closet,
how did you know so abruptly
that you and she could live expansively
in the little cage of loving?

Simple equation of 2=1 multiplying
the space for being to the power of infinity
All roots reaching to the same hidden flow
and all your fibers drinking

Lovers, plunge into this deep if it calls you.
Drown in the tide of self-losing.

Awakening in the tremor of your nuptials,
body to body, languor of self-conceiving,
you see all that you see is one
and one the all of your seeing.

HARMONY OF STAR AND DITCH

And in the case of superior things like stars, we discover a kind of unity in separation. The higher we rise on the scale of being, the easier it is to discern a connection even among things separated by vast distances.

MARCUS AURELIUS, *MEDITATIONS*

AQUIFER

When you have left everything and everything
has left you but the getting and giving of love
like the flow of pure water,
you will find the house you always longed to enter.

You expected labyrinths or a long snowy climb,
a dangerous river or a deep, deep descent,
decades of disciplined solitude
to gain the silent center.

All along you were on the threshold
in the noise of happy children,
in the sweet delta of their daily changing,
in that ferocious surge you felt to protect them.

What you always hoped to make the time to seek
was there in the maddening ecstasy as you clung
for dear life to the one who helped you make them,
artesian joy of two becoming single.

In the seepage of that dependence, body for body,
simple as the pull of earth to unseeable depths,
even the inlets and tributaries of your art are unneeded.
The long pursuit that you hoped at the end to have time for

is already perfect. The sea for which you always thirsted
has already filled and brought you
where you hoped one day to be, down deep
where you always were.

NOW IS ALWAYS

Now is always
a good time
to forgive the weather or a past mistake or fate
and to celebrate whatever mood
the moon has chosen to display
above the alley neon of the liquor store

Now is always
a good time
to forget the smoky insults of a friend
or to turn your irritating grudges into pearls
presenting them in eighteen karat settings to random strangers
on the twisty high noon boulevard of shards

Now is always
a good time
to recollect a favorite song or book
and tell your lover how it made you who you are
offering your nakedness like a compliment or a winter tree
or an open skid row bottle under the silver glory of the stars

AFTER READING SOME LATE POEMS
OF PABLO NERUDA

The red needle of his compass always holds
toward passion. His goal and bearing both,
to live in fire. Passion won and passion lost,
endured and abandoned.

                        And there was labor
along the way, admitting no necessity of grace
or meaning. Killing, too, without regret,
a law of earth since life began, without
which there is neither destiny nor dream.

On the continent he understood so well
and loved, he made an edifice for every form,
both gross and golden, indigenous all
with all their striving, noble, blind, or rotten.
A milky kiss is not a boon the poet seeks,
much less the politician. Blood and flowers,
flowers and blood, the world can spawn
a thousand Edens, a thousand thousand Armageddons.

All the while the self exists as plenitude
like proteins in our DNA, each single self
a string of selves, muck and lightning.
An insect self. A reptile self. Even a human self,
belonging to all, fiercely alight,
most fully alive in the latest years
as the body burns away its fever
and the architecture settles into ash.

Into the dithyramb of dying, when
the spirit crouches at the lowest note,
let the dying welcome gratitude

like the *mot juste,* as lost and weary men
rejoice to recognize a landmark or to see
again a long-grieved comrade. In her hand
the needle turns one final time. And so
we go. The heart's true north. Its natural pole.

ZOPHAR

Nor are you to be called instructors, for you have one instructor, the Messiah.

MATT 23:10 (NRSV)

In no particular order, my five best ways
to cure the blues: hold a baby, pray,
make love. That's three. The fourth is tear your clothes
then sit on the ground with a few of your friends and indulge
in a little rhetoric. But let the rhetorician
understand the risk of speech; blasphemies
ooze from the forked tongue of good intentions.
So often silence is the wisest mode
of argument, uplifting, healing where
dialectics or polemics wound.
Work hard—that's fifth. Wash, rake, serve, make something.

A sixth, if there can be that many on
a list of five, would be to sing. Let's say
that singing is implied in numbers four
and five. It is no stretch to claim it's both
a kind of rhetoric and work. To sing?
Of what? Of babies, God, the young and old
in love. That is, express the pain and joy
of life and living. Sometimes, as in this song,
I sing of singing, and I like to say
that every song is metasong.

I cannot claim that any song of mine
has forked the lightning, flared from nothingness
to dazzle primal and uncomprehending dark.
Like everyone down in the dust, stricken by love,
which costs so much, I grope for syntax

and mangle syllogisms. Bear this in mind,
whoever reads this book. Verily,
only One is wise. Therefore, I offer in advance
my seven rams and seven bulls. Yet even
if every measure and rhyme be born of blindness
down in the deepest pit of my desire,
I still believe my making holy work.
It is the darkest night that best reveals
the lightning and the stars.

PRESENT

The rabbit escaped
from my neighbor's hutch
a month ago.
Now she sprawls
and dozes
in my front yard,
sleek and black and limp
as an inner tube,
beside another neighbor's
sprawling, dozing
one-eyed Persian tomcat.
Strips of sycamore bark,
curled scraps
of papyrus,
blow onto my lawn
from our neighbor's lawn
on their way to other
neighbors' lawns.
The shadows
of the lyrical birds
draw hieroglyphs
on the grass,
which moment by moment
the brilliant sun
erases.
I have completed
another orbit.
Everything is a gift
in the making.

WEIGHTLESS

for the billionaires in space

Let the joy and sorrow of all
be all your sorrow and joy.
This is the way
to become weightless.

The pain and pleasure
that always held you down
propels you now.

Having exhausted all the stages of your flight,
at the extremity of your longing
deep in yourself
you thrust
against the gravity
of a dying planet
until you reach an altitude of freedom.

What you have come for
has come for you.

Tumbling and trembling
as you pass the sun
you see a dawn breaking
such as you never imagined.

Now floating in the atmosphere
of no return,
you realize a heaven
that can never be disturbed.

You are shredded into wholeness,
broken into being.

OF FORM AND THE FORMLESS

While they were eating, Jesus took a loaf of bread ...

MATT 26:26A (NRSV)

When the celebrant raises the host,
I see the nucleus of every atom.
I see the sun, primordial earth,
a pregnant womb.

I see an egg, an acorn, an embryo,
the iris of every eye,
a whole note of every anthem,
the wide-open mouth of a child.

Life sings and cries its incessant,
insatiable desire for delight.
Foxfire blooms from rotting wood
as the galaxy spirals in the shape of zero.

All that is made offers itself to unmaking.
I make a living paten of my hands
and receive my own little wafer,
a holy morsel tasting of nothing,

a wisp as dry as dust and ashes,
a hole punched through impermanence,
a portal of presence. It could be
anyone, everyone, everything.

DAUGHTER HEAVEN MOUNTAIN

To begin her yearly wellness exam,
Dolores is given three words
to remember, a test for dementia.

"Daughter." "Heaven." "Mountain."

Pulse oximeter. Blood pressure cuff.
Stethoscope sounding her torso
for the beat of her heart, the flow
of breath. "Have you recently fallen?"
Dr. Darby asks. "Do you have trouble
getting out of a chair? Trouble
with drooling? With swallowing?
Incontinence? Vision? Memory?"

Meanwhile, ageless Ni Zan,
the Yuan master, paints a perfect world
in her brain. In his signature way,
he uses only black ink and leaves
large swaths of the paper
untouched by the brush, suggesting
sky or mist or water.

From nothing
there emerges a bamboo grove
on a riverbank, plums and orchids
and gangly pines, a hermit's hut
tucked away in the cleft of a distant range
to prove the existence of humans.

Dolores learned long ago
how Ni Zan, in his last years,
gave away all that he owned

to take up the life of a Daoist wanderer
in the Lake Tai region of his youth.

Now she is straightening her blouse
as her doctor explains
the alarming numbers in her blood,
her prognosis and options.

To the doctor her smile as she listens
is disconcerting. Yet she hears
and understands, clearly, even
as she follows the wanderer,
the strokes of his brush.

Ni Zan leads her across
a rugged stream, under gaunt trees
with an owl perched on one high limb,
past a grassy swell where a doe
and fawn are browsing, into
a vast blank space,
where his brush pauses.

She knows she must travel through
on her way
to the far mountains drifting
in nothingness
below the untouched sky,
a tall mother mountain maternally rising
above her brood of little mountains.

"And now for the test," Dr. Darby says,
noticing her far-away look.
"What are the words
that I gave you to remember?"

Half in a mystic dream she meets his eyes
with her inscrutable smile.

"Daughter. Heaven. Mountain."

THE LAKE OF SERENITY

The stones named can't and won't
make no splash on the surface of Serenity.
This lake appears without shore or horizon.
It gathers every droplet into union,
and anyone who looks in it can see
what really is.

Bring no and must.
Bring did and forgot.
Bring better and best, worse and worst.
Bring your toys and all the refuse of excess.
Bring illness and injury, pride and shame.
Bring your prison, and bring your grave.

Bear them all as you walk on the water
to a coordinate you know. With a breath
let them fall, all at once.
However massive and heavy the heap,
it won't make a ripple on the surface,
it can't make a dent in the water.

Something big has swallowed it.
Something big is letting it go.
Be still in stillness as it sinks
toward the bottomless bottom, falls
and falls through crystal clarity,
through singular darkness

to a level too deep for salvage,
to a depth unknown to human vision
into Light beyond the world's light—
that original radiance, that corona, that core
in which all that is not itself must vanish,
from which all that is All arises.

THE PATH OF LOVE BEYOND LOVE

Only the word "I" divides me from God.

YUNUS EMRE, *THE DROP THAT BECAME THE SEA:*
LYRIC POEMS

In union there is no love,
for love depends on *I* and *other*,
subjects and objects, two or more.

The union I mean is not the unity
of many limbs on one tree
or cells in a particular leaf.

Nor the collective of notes
that makes a single symphony
complete.

Nor a thousand
harmonious utterances
of Allah, Amen, or Aum.

Rather, it is like the oneness
of silence, the ground of all sound
being perfect and indivisible.

The wellness you feel in this,
the wholeness—you might
call it love. Love beyond love.

Or happiness. Or peace.
Or utter beingness itself.
But really there isn't a word.

www.ingramcontent.com/pod-product-compliance
Lightning Source LLC
LaVergne TN
LVHW051646080426
835511LV00016B/2517